Illustrated by
Ron Broda

DINOSAUR
Digging Up a Giant

Written by
Chris McGowan

North Winds Press
A Division of Scholastic Canada Ltd.

To Cory, a young man with an enquiring mind.
— C. M.

To Dylan, the newest dinosaur in the Broda family.
— R. B.

The illustrations for this book were made with paper sculpture and watercolour. Each layer of paper was cut, formed and painted before being glued into place. The finished sculptures were then carefully lit and photographed to create the final images.

This book was designed in QuarkXPress, with type set in 17pt Catull medium.

Photography by William Kuryluk.

Canadian Cataloguing in Publication Data

McGowan, C., 1942-
Dinosaur : digging up a giant

ISBN 0-590-51509-8

1. Dinosaurs – Juvenile literature. I. Broda, Ron. II. Title.

QE862.D5M258 1999 j567.9 C99-930651-0

The words Gelvar and Frisbee are registered trademarks.

Text copyright © 1999 by Chris McGowan.
Illustrations copyright © 1999 by Ron Broda.
All rights reserved.

No part of this publication may be reproduced or stored in a retrieval system, or transmitted in any form or by any means, electronic, mechanical, recording, or otherwise, without written permission of the publisher, North Winds Press, a division of Scholastic Canada Ltd., 175 Hillmount Road, Markham, Ontario, Canada L6C 1Z7. In the case of photocopying or other reprographic copying, a licence must be obtained from CANCOPY (Canadian Copyright Licensing Agency), 1 Yonge Street, Suite 1900, Toronto, Ontario, M5E 1E5.

5 4 3 2 1   Printed and bound in Canada   9/9 0 1 2 3 4/0

What's this bone doing in your backyard? What animal does it come from? If it's a really old bone it could be from an Ice Age animal like a sabre-tooth cat or a mammoth. And if it's very, very old, it could even be a dinosaur! You'd have to dig it up and study it to answer all the questions about it. And that's exactly what scientists called paleontologists do.

Hot.

Hot and dry and lifeless.

But this area wasn't always lifeless.

The stark Alberta badlands are a perfect place for paleontologists to look for dinosaur bones. This paleontologist thinks she might have found a piece of bone from a dinosaur.

She chips and brushes away at the rock. The exposed bone is rounded, about the size of a clenched fist. As she digs deeper she realizes it's a leg bone, a femur.

More of the skeleton is found. But what sort of dinosaur is it?

From the size of the bone and its shape, the paleontologist thinks it might be a hadrosaur. Hadrosaurs, or duck-billed dinosaurs, fed on plants. There were many different sorts of hadrosaurs.

But it could also be a ceratopsian, or horned dinosaur, which had a bony frill extending back behind its skull.

The paleontologist will have to dig out more of the skeleton to find out.

A whole team of paleontologists goes to work. While one unearths more of the skeleton, another sketches the find and takes photographs.

Someone else squirts a liquid plastic called Gelvar onto the bone as it's uncovered. This gives it strength, so it won't break too easily.

This is the first time that anyone has ever seen these bones – and they don't belong to a horned dinosaur.

Now most of the skeleton is exposed. It is a hadrosaur, but until the skull is completely uncovered the scientists don't know what kind.

It might be a flat-headed one like *Anatosaurus*.

Anatosaurus was about 8 metres long. It lived 75 million years ago, during what's known as the Cretaceous Period.

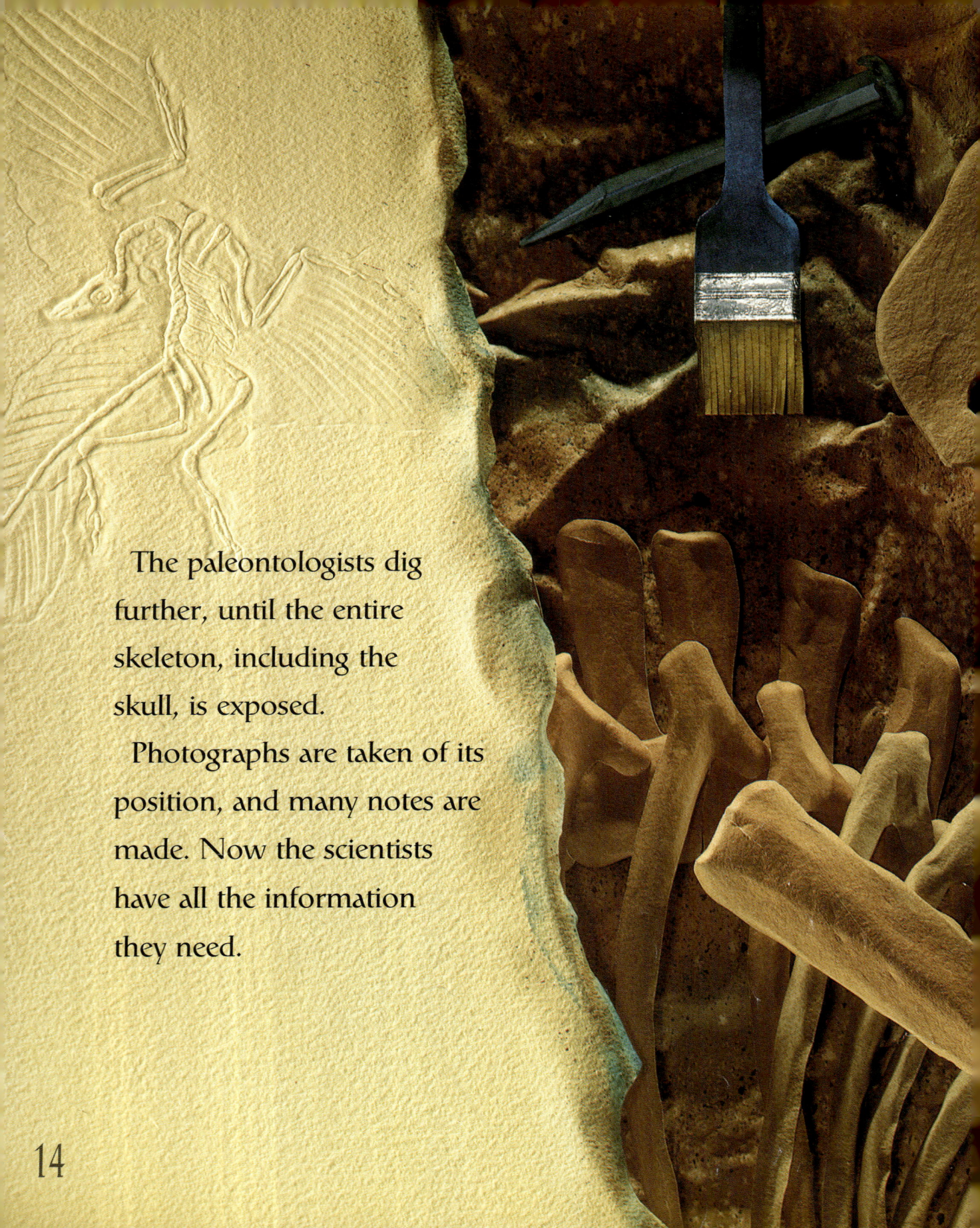

The paleontologists dig further, until the entire skeleton, including the skull, is exposed.

Photographs are taken of its position, and many notes are made. Now the scientists have all the information they need.

The shape of the skull tells them it can't be *Parasaurolophus,* because that hadrosaur had a much longer crest. Inside its crest was a long U-shaped tube that might have been used like a trombone for making loud honking sounds.

It's not *Edmontosaurus* either. *Edmontosaurus* had no crest at all.

The skeleton belongs to *Corythosaurus*. On its head was a hollow crest shaped like a Frisbee. When it breathed, the air took a loop through the crest to reach its throat.

Now that the *Corythosaurus* skeleton is exposed, it's time to get it back to the museum.

The bones are wrapped in layers of cloth dipped in
wet plaster and allowed to set, like a cast for a broken leg.
To make these field jackets is a lot of work:

A trench is chiselled out around a group of bones. The bones
are covered with tissue paper, then strips of burlap soaked in
plaster of Paris are spread over them, in layers. When the
plaster on top sets, the block is flipped over and plastered
on the other side.

When the plaster is dry the field jacket is labelled
using a felt-tipped marker. This shows which
skeleton it is, and where this block fits
in with all the others.

After the completed field jackets are transported to the museum, paleontologists start to work on the skeleton in the laboratory. The field jackets are opened, and rock is carefully removed from the bone, using special tools. The bones are strengthened with more Gelvar, and any breaks are repaired with glue. The bones are then ready for study, and for building into a skeleton.

The technicians are skilled at their jobs. They have already built a number of dinosaurs in the dinosaur gallery.

They're also working on a gallery of mammals from the Ice Age. The biggest skeleton is a mammoth.

Mammoths, which are related to elephants, lived over 10,000 years ago. They had thick coats to help keep warm. Sabre-tooth cats were meat eaters. They had extra-long teeth for attacking their prey.

Technicians have been working on the *Corythosaurus* skeleton for many months now. They attach the bones to a steel framework. It has to be strong, because the bones are heavy. The technicians have to make sure they keep all the bones in the right order and position.

How did this *Corythosaurus* die? Maybe it was preyed upon by a *Tyrannosaurus rex*.

Long-necked plesiosaurs like *Hydrotherosaurus* lived in the sea.

Giant pterosaurs like *Pteranodon* might have been flying overhead.

We can't be sure how this one dinosaur died. But more than a year after a little bit of bone peeked out from a rock, the paleontologists and technicians have made *Corythosaurus* live again!

You wanted to know . . .

What colour were the dinosaurs?

We are often asked what colour dinosaurs were, but we have no way of knowing. We do know what the skin of some dinosaurs looked like, though — for example, hadrosaurs had pebbly skin. Natural casts were formed when a dinosaur's body pressed into the ground where it lay, leaving an impression. This natural impression (mold) became filled with sand, whose grains became stuck together, forming a natural sandstone cast of the original skin.

How do we know what kinds of plants were around when the dinosaurs lived?

Plants left their fossils behind in the rocks too, but most of our information comes from microscopic pollen grains — those pesky things that give us hay fever. Each plant species has its own distinctive-looking pollen grain. By grinding up rock samples and dissolving them with strong acid, paleontologists can extract the pollen grains and study them under the microscope. They can be compared with living species and identified, giving us a good idea of what plants were around when the dinosaurs lived.

Can you tell from the bones if a dinosaur was a boy or a girl?

We can't be sure, but we sometimes have clues. In *Tyrannosaurus*, for example, some skeletons are large and chunky while others are smaller and more slender. It is thought that the larger skeletons are the females. In the same way, the skeletons of female birds of prey, like eagles and hawks, are larger and heavier than those of the males. For our own species it is the other way around, and men are bigger-boned than women.

Why are so many dinosaur remains found in Alberta?

In parts of Alberta, especially around Drumheller, conditions were just right for the bones of the dinosaurs to be preserved after they died. Excellent preservation requires rapid burial. Otherwise the bones are soon broken up by scavengers. There were lots of dinosaurs living around Drumheller 75 million years ago, and lots of rivers. If a dinosaur drowned crossing a river, its body would sink and become covered up by silt.

How do you say it?

Anatosaurus (ah-NA-toh-SAWR-us)
ceratopsian (sare-a-TOP-see-un)
Corythosaurus (COR-ith-o-SAWR-us)
Cretaceous (kree-TAY-shus)
Edmontosaurus (ed-MON-toh-sawr-us)
Gelvar (gel-vuhr)

hadrosaur (HAD-ro-sawr)
Hydrotherosaurus (HY-dro-THEYR-oh-SAWR-us)
paleontologist (PAY-lee-ahn-TOL-oh-jist)
Parasaurolophus (par-ah-sawr-OL-oh-fus)
Pteranodon (ter-AN-oh-don)
Tyrannosaurus rex (tye-RAN-oh-SAWR-us rex)